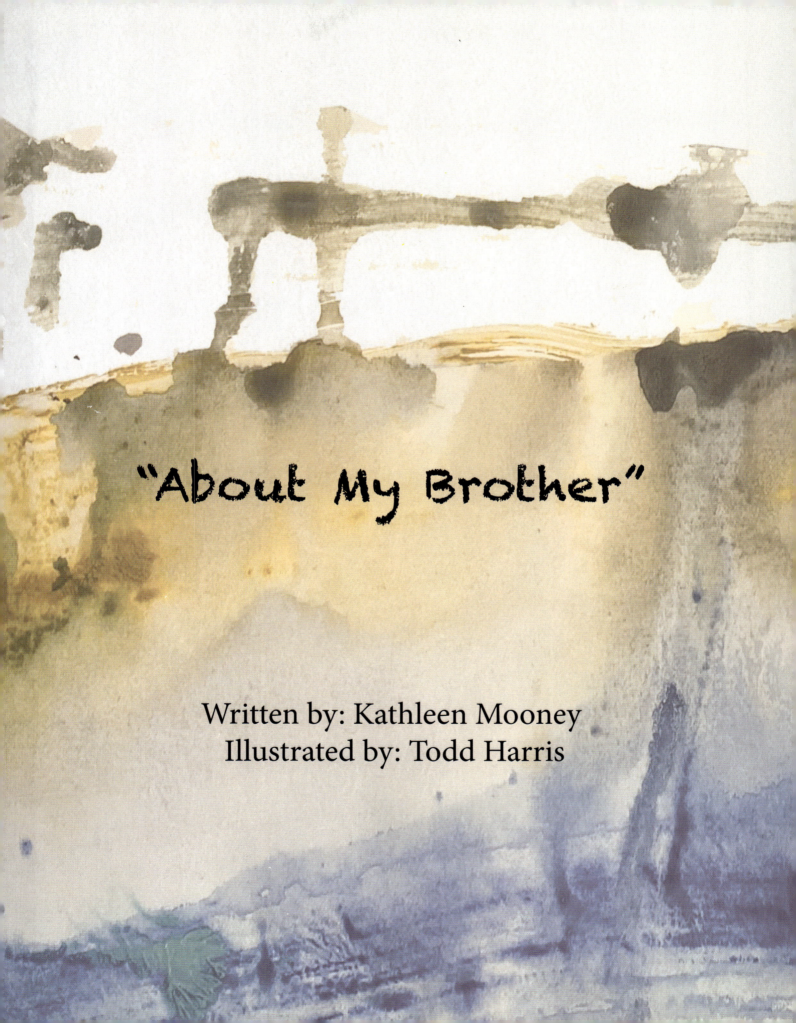

"About My Brother"

Written by: Kathleen Mooney
Illustrated by: Todd Harris

Dedicated to Mom, Dad, Tim and Kevin, my first, best and favorite teachers.

Also dedicated to my role models, Roberta Davenport and Reese Scott.

You see, the thing is... Kevin is different.

When he talks, it kinda sounds like he is underwater, or there are marbles in his mouth.

His words come out slow like the last drop of honey dripping from the jar...

Most people can't even understand what he is saying...

...and puddles of drool sometimes dribble from his chin like a slow, leaky, drooly faucet.

Kevin wears an eye patch over one eye, it helps the other eye see better...

But sometimes people say he looks like a PIRATE.

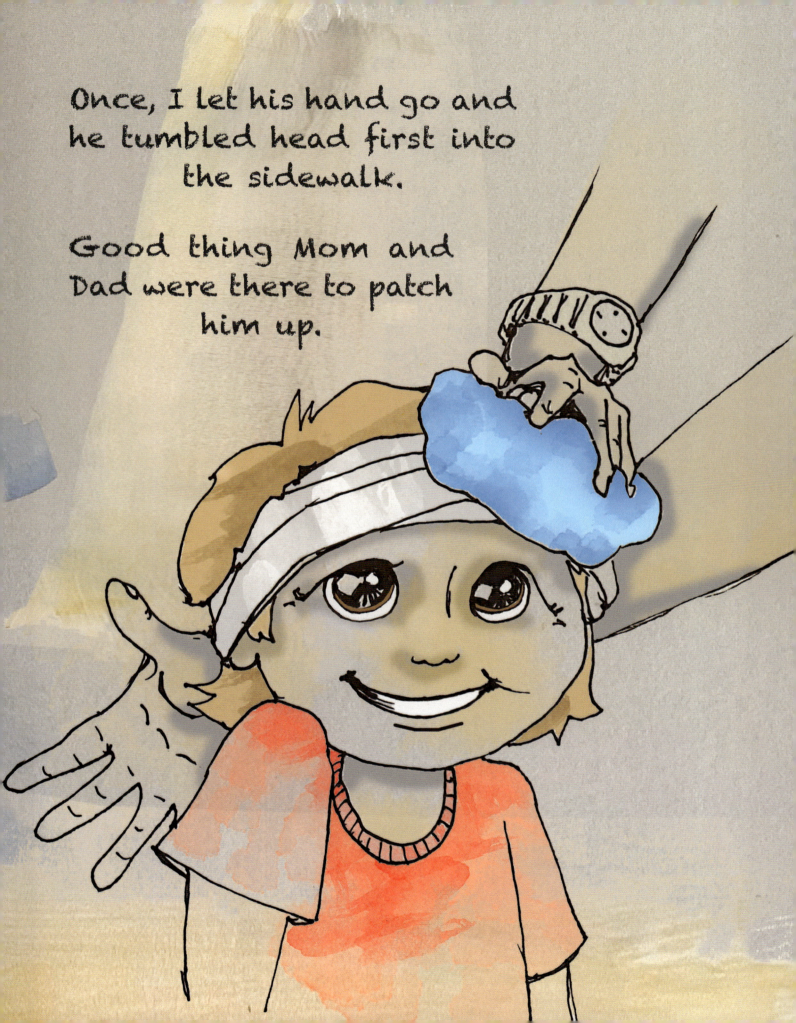

Mom and dad explain to us that Kevin gets so many presents to play with at home because the other kids never ask him to play.

One snowy day when school was canceled, Tim, Kevin and I piled our snowsuits on and trudged carefully across the snowy street. Some of Kevin's classmates were in the middle of a snowball fight.

"Hey! Can Kevin play too?" Tim asked, interrupting the group of kids mid-throw.

"Uh...um....nnnooo...my mom just said we have to go inside now." replied one of the kids as the group quickly turned and walked away toward their house.

Disappointed, we turned around and went home.

A few minutes later, Kevin's classmates were back outside playing in the snow.

On family bowling nights Kevin loves to bowl all by himself. Once, when it was his turn, Kevin looked back at us with a grin then tossed the bowling ball down lane next to ours...twice!

I'm pretty sure he did it on purpose.

Long car rides give Kevin a chance to sing along to his favorite songs. It's not long before Tim and I join in and our singing turns into shrieking fits of laughter.

We have a secret contest to see who will be the first to get on mom and dad's nerves. Kevin is always the winner.

One of Kevin's favorite pastimes is to see how quickly he can drive our dad up a wall. His favorite tactic is repeating the same thing over and over and over until...Dad sees red!

The last thing you should know about Kevin is that he will probably ask you for a hug. He might get a little drool on your shirt...I hope that's ok.

My mom will help clean it off.

So now that you know about my brother, are you ready to come in and meet Kevin?

Traumatic Brain Injuries

Traumatic brain injury (TBI) is a sudden injury to the brain through a blow, fall, or jolt to the body or head. It is also referred to as Cerebral Palsey post-birth. Brain injuries can be mild and last a short time, or they can be severe and last a lifetime, like Kevin's. Most people with a TBI lose some of their ability to walk, run, move or talk, for a short time, or for the rest of their lives, as in Kevin's case. They may forget everything they learned before the TBI and have to start over from scratch. This can take many years and many people along the way to work with the individual and their families to help the person injured do simple things they used to do on their own, such as get dressed, brush their teeth or even feed themselves. A brain injury can also cause a person to have seizures or tremors (uncontrollable shaking of limbs, hands or feet), life-long challenges that Kevin deals with everyday. TBIs can change the way people look, think, move, behave and sound but they don't diminish the person who was injured! This is how Kevin was affected - his brain and body changed, but his personality has always been the same, sweet, kind and funny! Most TBI victims still enjoy the same things others enjoy, such as being with family, going to birthday parties and doing normal day to day activities like going to the movies or out for an ice cream sundae.

For more information / help support:

The Brain Injury Association of America https://www.biausa.org.

This book can be used at home or in the classroom as a great introduction for:

Trauma informed instruction
Social Emotional Learning - empathy, compassion and acceptance
Diverse families
Small moments
Similes and metaphors
Figurative language
Character analysis
Past, present and future
Flashbacks as story elements
Students from grades pre-k - grade 8 and beyond will benefit from reading and discussing concepts addressed this book

Discussion Questions, Coordinating Depth of Knowledge (DOK) levels

Page 5 - 6
What is different about Kevin?
Why does the narrator tell the reader that Kevin is "different"?
(DOK level 1, 2)

Page 7-8
Why are people staring at Kevin?
How do you think Kevin's sister feels when Kevin knocks things over?
How do you think it makes the narrator or Kevin feel when strangers stare at them? How might you feel?
(DOK level 2)

Page 11 - 12
Why did Kevin's siblings say "it's not fair" when opening their Christmas presents?
How do you think they felt when Kevin received more presents than they did?
Describe a time you felt like Kevin's brother or sister?
Why did Kevin's parents give him the most presents?
(DOK levels 1, 2 and 3)

Page 13 -14
How did Kevin's classmates not show empathy toward Kevin?
What would you do differently if you were Kevin's classmate?
(DOK level 4)

Page 15 - 16
How did Kevin's brother and sister feel after Kevin's friends wouldn't play with him?
How do you think it made Kevin's siblings feel when he was rejected by his classmates?
How do you think being rejected by his classmates made Kevin feel?
(DOK level 2)

Page 17
Why do you think Kevin threw the bowling ball down the wrong lane?
How do you think his siblings reacted when tossed the bowling ball down the wrong lane twice?
(DOK level 2)

Page 18
What do the siblings do in the car to have fun?
How do you and your siblings (or friends) have fun?
(DOK level 1)

Page 21 -22 Would you go into the house to play? Why or why not?
(DOK level 3)

Beyond the text

What adjectives would you use to describe Kevin? (DOK level 2 and 3)

How is your family similar to Kevin's? How is it different? (DOK 2)

Describe Kevin's relationship with his sister? How is it similar or different to the relationship he has with Tim? (DOK level 2)

Would you like to be Kevin's friend? Why or why not? (DOK level 3)

Who do you relate to most in this story? Explain your reasoning. (DOK level 4)

What does loneliness look like to you? (DOK level 1 and 2)

Why is the narrator telling the reader about Kevin before they come over? (DOK level 2,) How would the story be different if the narrator never told you about Kevin before the reader comes over to play? (DOK level 3)

What hardships does Kevin face? (DOK levels 2 and 3)

If you could change the ending, how would you change it? (DOK level 4)

If you had a chance to meet Kevin, what would you ask him? What would you tell him? What would you ask his sister? (DOK level 3)

What was the symbolism of the cat found throughout the book? (DOK level 4)

What was the author's purpose? How do you know? (DOK level 3)

How does Kevin's family show they love him? How does your family show each other love? (DOK level 3)

What is theme/themes of this book? How do you know? (DOK level 3)
Themes

Author Bio

Kathleen Mooney (Katie) is a literacy coach, early childhood literacy specialist, and teacher with a passion for art, education, and boxing. She is also a dog mom to a playful little terrier named Finleigh. Her love of art ignited the first time she picked up a crayon and started drawing at her parent's kitchen table at the age of three. This passion led her to earn her B.F.A. from Pratt Institute in 2001. Katie traded in her crayons for a chalkboard and followed her heart to the classroom to become an early childhood teacher in 2006. She was inspired to write her first children's book, About My Brother, after teaching for many years in Brooklyn, NY. Katie found it challenging to find stories and texts that feature the experiences of coming of age with a family member with special needs. Many of her students are in families much like her own. She hopes that this book will reach families of children with and without special needs and serve as a tool to help destigmatize different abilities, promote social inclusion, and foster empathy. When she's not writing, drawing, or coaching, you will find Katie side-stepping and counter-punching in boxing gyms or at her local park in Brooklyn, supervising Finleigh's squirrel chases.

Illustrator Bio

Todd O. Harris, is an illustrator and artist based in Atlanta. He is an alumnus of Pratt Institute where he learned graphic design along with earning a BA in industrial design. His artwork comes from a love of beautiful things, unique objects, furniture, and modern architectural design. Todd's love of comics, children books, fables, and short stories, however, are what led him to want to illustrate. His illustrations are drawn freehand on paper combined with the use of watercolor, ink, and graphic design, to express a loose handmade quality to his work. Find Todd and his artwork online at Todd Oscar Design, website: www.toddoscar.com.